A Troubadour's Thread

Sanya Osha

Langaa Research & Publishing CIG
Mankon, Bamenda

Publisher:
Langaa RPCIG
Langaa Research & Publishing Common Initiative Group
P.O. Box 902 Mankon
Bamenda
North West Region
Cameroon
Langaagrp@gmail.com
www.langaa-rpcig.net

Distributed in and outside N. America by African Books Collective
orders@africanbookscollective.com
www.africanbookcollective.com

ISBN: 9956-790-99-0

© Sanya Osha 2013

DISCLAIMER
All views expressed in this publication are those of the author and do not necessarily reflect the views of Langaa RPCIG.

Preface

During the final stages of putting together this volume and preparing it for publication I was asked in an interview if academic writing was different from creative writing. In my view, the two forms of writing couldn't be more different. While academic writing has to deal with a host of disciplinary and stylistic constraints, creating writing on the other hand, strives in its purest form, for unfettered expression. Some of my exact words were, "imaginative writing, for me, should strive for utter freedom of expression and hence it should confront as much as possible the shackles of censorship, both external and self-imposed. Imaginative writing should be precisely what it purports to be, which is, an act of pure imagination. Going by this understanding, it also becomes an essentially transgressive type of activity, or preferably, an act of subversion".

The present volume, *A Troubadour's Thread*, emerged after a long and haphazard quest to reach poetic maturation. I had started writing as a poet and "finding one's voice" wasn't as easy as I had thought it would be. Although I had always struggled to arrive at, and experience, that somewhat mystical creative transformation, it didn't often come when I had expected it or how I had anticipated it. Similar to fluctuations and rhythms associated with birth, the creation of this volume followed its own evolutionary path seemingly independent of my own often strenuous efforts.

A Troubadour's Thread emerged as a journey, a discovery as well as an arrival at an unforced evolutionary state. It is where I find myself within the least unconstrained seam of poetic expression. This state seized me at a precise moment of writing and continued until the verses were complete and there is, one hopes, a unity of theme, mood and tone.

Sanya Osha,
Pretoria,
April, 2013

And the winds here are crying
For immobile planets
Where they can go dark
Amid their own fortress...

I go from water to air
And back to water
Slowly twisted by the night
Until disturbed beyond all
I begin to wish an iron claw
Would drain all the blood.

A small angered bird
Has drawn spite into my garden
In his eyes I see the cunning
Of a mind forced to rave,
A machine he rides sings a tune
Love has begun to yield to...

And when I open my mouth
To address the night-sea people
Birds flutter out of my voice
All trembling to die with little trace
Upon an horizon of dusk;
Nightly I stand convulsed with night
Hoping the sun would not poison
The dark tumour at dawn.
And she sits in front of me
Making plans for the night;
A black gem in the forehead
Of the formless whirling dark...
My own universe is possessed by clouds

In my shirt sleeves I make stitches
For a more tolerable future
Knitting together islands of weeping clouds
And then embalming them with night.

I have begun to stitch
Together dead white birds,
They had sung to me in death
About love and song
Robbing them of all judgement,
Amid a colony of wild spectators
I have been called
To take night to the heart of a song
I have been given
The flesh of dead birds
To make a symphony of blackened diamonds.

Stilled winds have to steady the voice
So that when it speaks
The mark would be engraved
Like when a rat runs hurriedly
Into a blank wall to make a cipher.

And then the gates are opened again...
Soulless feathers cry feverishly
After a heart
Night muslins crying for lack of weight
What a pain to know
That even the night too
Can sometimes go weak.

And in disembowelled form
All our foibles become visible
Pale, like misted mirrors
And beings in flesh
Make heavy-footed resolutions
And just like whitened scree
They roll away with sureness
Over the mud fences beyond.

And from the voice,
The flesh has been taken away
And the halo of it
Hangs like an impaled animal
In a limbo of passive soulless light
And within the void of a scream
Silence makes a distorted
And horrific orifice,
The rent beak of the bird
Of the dead sphere.

And within the long room of the chest
We settled all the philosophic
Armoury we could muster;
To make it worthwhile
We placed them upon the cushions of night
And then in a fever of oblivion
The breezes of a music
Came and proclaimed nothing was.

Upon my deceptive heath
I had planted mahogany trees
Which had sprouted

Like innocuous tumours
Over acres of dream
And a flute came within me
Undressed herself and then
Left within a blank page.

What a lesson to reach
This white empty room
Where all illusions become iron-grey,
I murdered a whole country
Of virgins in their sleep
To realise that the luminosity
Of golden affection
Tears off the chords
Of legs and voices steeped in iron.

At the threshold of a tyrannical wisdom
I hear the rustlings of a chick:
After a quarter of a century
Filled to the rim with heart
A tome of tears threatens
To give to the heart a song.

On the first forgiving night
I shall go again to mend
With a dark cement, the violated promise
That I've built out of many starvations
And in the erstwhile cluttered room
A pleasure the most loved one created
Has torn down all defences.

Trying as hard as rocks
Upon a plinth in mid-sky
I amalgamate half-formed thoughts
Like a sage undressing
Within gowns of clouds
And water-logged from the inside
I begin to count
How many steps the spirit has taken.
And among the relics of a lecherous age
She has managed to relive a profane moment
Laughing like a virginal nymph
And even with the corpulence of sin
We have given to decadence
A luminous wave of love.

When she saw that he had
Lost all his elements again
To a catastrophe of light-headed love
She gathered night about her
And like a panther upon her haunches
She strove to make a man
Of him again.

And she too became poisoned
By his inflammation
Which donned her with her infantile pinafore
And she became more inflamed
Than even him with a malady
That was more potent
Than the most seductive
Stirrings of dawn.

The sadness of our interminable seasons
Says that rage is not for this house
For each time we raise a just argument
A thin flute carries off a small note
Which it humiliates sharply
On a coast of ridicule and oblivion.

In front of a host of guardian angels
Who would soon become serpents
The anchor leaves the anchorage
And within the shelves
That have served as our fortress,
An ambiguous breeze
Waltzes away with our vein of sorrow

And when we found out
That we were not even broken
But were as irresolute
As the air of open spaces
We began to drink concentratedly again
Out of the heavy cistern of night.

Coming to realise that sterility
May assuage the flight of blood
We begin to wear the bone of age
With a method worthy of the silver
Room the moon grants us.
Debussy makes his entry
His locks waves of embryonic motion
For a piece can only be this beautiful
And the moon drinks feverishly
From the shores of his hair.

And the woman of the ocean's
Most organic stomach
Appears without a bone
And dissolves without a trace,
Incessantly,
While the moon slithers up
To shower upon those locks and shores
The soft rays of kisses and tears.

The courtyard which we neglected
To acquire the glory
Of the oriental habit
Like a mural clouded by gloom
Suddenly declares a carnival
Without regard for the approach of dawn
And all the birds of our previous night
Make yesterday's wine
Into this morning's creatures of fiesta.

The evening has not arrived
When the mountain ranges
Would bear us from its will
And set within us eyes that are closed but seeing
And a wisdom shrouded by silence
And between the howling death below
And the imminent fire,
A film of eternity
Shall unravel white vapours from us.

And she seeing that nothing
But butterflies nurture him,
She put all her mercies into a trunk

And headed for frontiers ravaged by war
While he began to mouth his miseries
First into the skies and then
Unto the dark mountains
That fed him with the sediment of night
To keep the air out of his blood.

It is his sunshine
That draws her to the pond
Which is the gallery of his dreams
For how else can one explain
The reason the likes of her
Slaughter him each time
They drink from the glow
Of the pond.
On learning his radiance
Was so contagious he began
To seek only thickets
With a functional luxuriance
And rooms the ghosts
Of bygone sages haunt
Until they became grey.

The fire eating his ankles
Is the cause of his most painful losses
For at every threshold of ecstasy
A longing takes him away
From the serene waves he should crave for
And deposits him
Like a redundant relic
Upon infernal banks of misery
Alone, without her.

To drain the malaise in his happiness
He began to scatter his seeds and roots
In coarse relentless soil
So that when he finally returns
His heart to the inconsolable tempests
It would be the light-house
In the aftermath of his youth.

His self-violated sanctuary
He cleaned out
And with the handling of one
Who had known the plagues
Of the bay of pestilence
He began to station the sacraments
His very scars had acquired
Within his semi-darkness...

He took a path
To his ancestral forest
And there within the clearing
In the valley
He found the man who had played
His flute before anyone else
Bent over the ancestral pond
And the image of his smile
Kept corroding his very being
And then he ran to the nearest mahogany
And struck it down
After which the forests began to chime his name.

Out of the dismembered winds
He found the grey tower

That rose out of the sea nightly
To brood high amongst the stormclouds
And naked nymphs plagued by lust
Came to swoon beside
The self-possessed railings
Only to be revived and consecrated
Like nuns by dawn.

And it was revealed
After a series of self-same deaths:
Bear the name of your tree
Like the soul clings to the body
Wear the trunk until bloodless,
It speaks through your voice
Live in the name of the tree
To the lowest pit of shame.

It wasn't that those planets
Never had light, light was always present
And light confused the configurations
With the unanchored
Revelry of ghosts
Whose floating lights
Drugged the young plant
Far more than twelve harvests.

Every line of verse
Purged the pain of its subtle power
And after the ablution
A shell which became the relic
Began to write into the bosom
Of the tumultuous night-sea

The lives of those who headed
Towards unmarked graves at sea-bottom.
Like the sands of a forgotten beach.

He made his heart a spacious tomb
And gave her a chair
Upon which to sit within it
And she began to scatter
Her wild cravings around the room
Until she noticed that the walls
Neither bulged nor eavesdropped,
He put his hand into his stomach
To feel his heart
But it was no longer there.

The gestures of cloud, wind, water
And at the most lapidarian of times, serpent
Becomes languorous in the labyrinth
Of a flooded memory
And with the resoluteness
Of a benign potentate
He begins to engrave
His thoughts and gestures into a range of stone.

He went into the hall of heroes
And there,
He found monumental presences
Carving up the air with invisible hands
And amid the obstacles
Of unconscious idolisers, he made a stairway
To mount the pyramids
With a lyre perched upon his lap.

When he asked a man
Whose jaws were hewn from marble
How a hurricane came to possess
The lances of his voice
He replied by dipping an index finger
Into a pot of fire
Until it glowed with a red flame
And with that very finger
He inscribed into a sacred tablet,
A hieroglyph.

After we had cemented the triumvirate
In a garden of elixirs
One of us out of a sudden
Inexplicable craving for feathers
Was seized by a paroxysm
Of stones and heartless eyes
And then we too began
To put on the feathers we never really had
And never again to resume the tactless smile.
He has to keep shifting
The cyclone of his desire
From lever to lever
Because he could never tell
What sea-level she may decide
To make the dots of her form
And with the precision
Of an illusionist he has to ride
His cyclone within many climes
And with one breath.

Gratitude had been the plague
Of a row of flowers
He tended on a hermetic acre
For yearly, sentimental floods
Flow back into his hard-won dryness
And so with a pair of shears
He began to trim those soft edges
Of their profuseness
Until sands of the sun
Littered the ground.

And when she came to know
That he had not killed
Every one of his butterflies
She began to undress
The body of his soul with her deepest eyes,
With a generosity that betrayed
Her disillusionment
And then she took him to a ledge
So he could throw himself
Into the turmoil of the night
Until it drained him of all his insects.

Stranded upon a dismal harbour
A row of flowers mourn him
From the depths of sunset sorrow
They mourn him for the boats
He had missed bearing delights,
Cornucopias for short-sighted princes
Who had never really needed them
At the height of their glory and sorrow.

On his bed which no one
Has taken any notice of
Shadows come to reel
With a plethora of unreal waltzes
And within the hallow of every sound
Waters of the night's turmoil
Flow to the lethal silences
And far from her mansion
A solitary phantom keeps vigil.

On reading her life of waters
I wanted to carry the heirloom
Of her departing ripple,
To use it to kiss in a full moon
I wanted each and every one
Of her silent syllables
To bulge before my eyes,
I wanted to forget
She had misty eyes.

And she can be seen
Inside her dissolving moon
Rendering its toxins impotent,
Within the worlds in her eyes
Footmarks fringed with blood
Lead into the desert
And the eyes say
She would never draw out the claws
And there within the desert
In her eyes
Bloodless souls continue to roam.

She made the moon her pen
And her river her paper
And a sage who became an imbecile
On account of the miracle
Began to howl down the desert
Unwinding in her eyes
So he would be allowed
To reach her pantheon
Without carrying along
The burden of his mind.

He'd rather she suffer
A thousand betrayals
Than enter into the wishing
Of his highway, bearing only
The emptiness of a sun...
She should be within the frozen storm
Whose greenish-grey hue
Still clouds the wisdom of her cemetery
So that visible thoughts
Would linger in the very eyes of her trees.

And I left the tumour
To flower and grow
In my ancestral mausoleum
Feeding on the cancer of its own secrets
And arresting the wind of its own ghosts
For its own dark embers
And the growths acquired from the curse
A magic we had never imagined.

As he could not be the stevedore

Of one brutal October night
As he could not impale her
With a frank nameless love
Upon the precipice
Of a near uninhabitable land
She shut him out of the door
Of her ageing to enjoy
The sour liquid of her solitude alone.

On knowing that the blindness of his winds
Had blown away entire paradises
He caught her at the most scalding moment
Of her transient glory
Pledging that he had enough iniquity
Within his hot and livid ribcage
To make the dark sea-mountain
Brood entire universes just for her.

Nature had made a river
The custodian of his manhood
And the knowledge of this
Became his most expansive grief
And then one night, he stole away
To pull the twin testicles
Of a mountain from the womb
Right to the crown
And the moon seeing this
Grew jealous and took to her heels.

There is a certain man
Incapable of becoming old
With a venomous family of bastard sons

Who threw fire onto his indifferent loins
And when he decided
Not to decide any longer
He became the underbelly of a river
Swine and perverse mares
Befouled at will.

Since he wanted to endure
The gloom inside a teardrop
And not its garish light
First, he swallowed whole, a tomb
And then he began to plant
Dense rows of tropical trees
And witch-doctors who had known
Too much of death,
Who had the old plantations
Of a forgotten sea
Swinging slowly within their pupils
Were conjured to tend them.

After weeding the whole circle
Of an eerily enchanted moon
After having been dazed
By whole leagues of ephemeral brilliances
The angered bird appears again
Dragging a syndrome of regret
Here, to the ground.

He took the mother-of-pearl handle
Of his adolescent voice
And dipped it in vitriol
And with it his hunger for her

And his craving to know
From the heart of the statute,
He took the hunger in his voice
And appeased it amid the epic ruins of man
That the birds of it
Would no longer go out
Into the forlorn horizons to die.

Like frightening winds
I feel presentiments of her coming
Dragging behind her
A whole garrison of dead men
An omen that knows her quite well
Brings her unobtrusively in his direction
And knowing she keeps a scythe
For those whose love hasn't grown
As deep as the night
I have begun to drink
Of the dense pool of night
To be its most faithful magician
And to wear layers upon layers of night
Until every cranny of my being
Becomes a sorcerer's dream.

Having suffered so many
Deaths and resurrections
Outside the door to the mysteries
A mysterious hand let him in
And therein he found vast halls
Littered with straw
And mists carrying no beginnings
Continued to drink from his soul

And so he made for the most shadowed niche
Where upon a mound of earth
He began to fill the room of his soul
With cemetery soil and twigs
To become the heart of mystery itself.

He pulled his north, south,
West and east gusts together
In an intense soundless kiss
That became a lodestone
For all his inane dissonances.

It should be a sphere of air
Fastidiously rolled upon the tongue
Or clay upon the sensitive
Hands of a sculptor
Not the lyrical shard of a broken mirror
Displaying more lives than one.

In him is the grown man, his soul
Out of the high blood tide engulfing me
Beyond men, beyond the realm of gods:
What way do your waves now move?
His essences are ridden with the arch man
I know blood calling the dark
You are the son of the wavering dusk
I hear the soul calling above the ruins
Does it enter into the crust
With the sun trying to meet you?

A rage that exhausted him
Ferried him out of the ordinary

Through a stairway of breezes
And there in an idyll
That had shed the weight of hope and prayer
A rootless shaman sat in lotus position
And without a word
He knew without seeing
That there were more stages
The journeying soul had to scale.

The indifference of no particular wind
Appropriates the stone of his soul
For no particular reason
And he has to endure the limbo
Of a very particular world
Until a cyclone carries him up
To the apex of its arresting presence.

And this is what he has been trying to accomplish
That all the air and straw of the universe could not grant...
Night shrunken to a little sphere
Enwrapped with the feathers of strange birds
Upon a mountain more enduring than death
And there he begins to atone for the crimes
Of father and mother, brother and sister,
And his night ensconced in plumes and feathers
Became a satellite onto itself.

He left the delirium of flesh
Finding it too exacting to maintain
For his wild brother to tend
And on getting to the spirits' abode

He found rituals of nakedness, the regimen
Beyond graves, beyond unmastered spirits.

And the anger, the anger of burst beings
Strips the dead of their peace
Strips pilgrim souls of their place
In stable plains
That if a despot were to emerge
From the drift of their realm
He would quench all the rootless fires
In the besieged kingdom.

Climbing the rungs where the brooms of heaven
Were sweeping in cryptic time
He passed souls that had been stranded
By their own wills
So he looked in the tunnel
That broke dark waves with light within him
To see if there were any footholds
To move higher.

Upon his brain dead birds
Within his pain dead birds
And then a resolution
Blows from nowhere
With which he begins
To stitch together with the charms
Of a night he had long discarded
That those slain even when dead
Would no longer sink
In their own fetid tears.

He places the flute made of blood
Which is a pump
Upon his lip,
Looks into the verdant sky
That drops pregnant with song
He blows the spiders out of the flute
And throws it into a disarray
Of sheets hovering in the green
Knee high air
To become the seed of an eternal garden.

He brought out his voice
Which is a ball of air
And rolled it slowly within his palm.
He brought the twig of his voice
And a wind came and blew it away
So he went down within his tomb
Down the dark steps
To his hard-edged desire
And the hairs of his night-wind
Started to cheer with the world.

My will which is partially agreed
To renounce nothing
Is like a sphere of crystal
Tucked away in a space
Of silent chaos
And on some days a pair of slit yellow eyes
Comes to rave to it
About the importance of being a red hot blade
Lodged in a meaningless black hole.

www.ingramcontent.com/pod-product-compliance
Lightning Source LLC
Chambersburg PA
CBHW012231230426
43666CB00040B/2905